15 MARKET RESEARCH MISTAKES TO AVOID

How to succeed using market research?

Ambarish Verma

न हि ज्ञानेन सदृशं पवित्रमिह विद्यते।

Here in this world there is nothing as pure or sublime as knowledge.

—SHREEMAD BHAGAWAD GEETA, CHAPTER 4, VERSE 38

This book is dedicated to my parents who have always guided my path and made me what I am today. I would also like to thank all my teachers who helped me satiate my curiosity with answers I couldn't have figured out on my own.

I would also extend my sincere thanks to my wife who has been at my side not only as a life partner but also as a true friend.

CONTENTS

INTRODUCTION

Without data you're just another person with an opinion.
—W. Edwards Deming

After being involved with marketing research projects for over a decade, I have seen my fair share of mistakes made by businesses, entrepreneurs and government organizations when conducting market research studies. Many a times organizations make some basic mistakes which often results in their poor satisfaction from market research. I have listed these mistakes in order of which they need to be addressed while commissioning any new market research study. I hope this list proves helpful to you in maintaining your faith in market research process.

MISTAKE 1: NOT CLEARLY DEFINING BUSINESS AND RESEARCH OBJECTIVES

Research is formalized curiosity. It is poking and prying with a purpose.
– Zora Neale Hurston

This is the most obvious mistake which often is given least attention. Like in computer science we say garbage in, garbage out (GIGO), similarly if you fail to define your business problems which you wish to solve and research objectives you wish to achieve via market research it's not going to produce meaningful results.

Business problem identification is the most important aspect. To get this right you need to discuss and brainstorm with all stakeholders who are going to get benefitted when this business problem is solved. Once you are clear what you wish to achieve out of a market research study, it can efficiently be converted into research objectives by your market research agency.

MISTAKE 2: CONDUCTING A WIDE COVERAGE MARKET RESEARCH STUDY WITH LOW DEPTH

It is not that I'm so smart. But I stay with the questions much longer.
- Albert Einstein

Many organizations while planning for market research study take inputs from all departments involved. Imagine a scenario where marketing director of a mid-size firm sends memo to all people in marketing a sales department of various product/service verticals to suggest business problems to be covered in proposed market research study. The result will be too many unrelated requests pouring in from each business vertical. This often results in them preparing a request for proposal (RFP) for market research study which tries to find answers of too many questions from a single study.

You may think what's wrong in trying to find answers for as many questions as possible via single study? Let me assure you that it's a recipe for disaster. Market research studies are not cheap to conduct and every question that needs answering may require use of different methodologies and research tools which can inflate the price of the market research thus reducing the feasibility of the project.

To cut corners and keep such projects under budget you may need to tone down the depth of the study e.g. reducing sample size for interviews, conducting less focus groups, focusing of less number of regions and markets etc. This will result in a market research study offering too little actionable information to solve any of the business problems you wished to solve.

MISTAKE 3: POOR BUDGET PLANNING

I believe in innovation and that the way you get innovation is you fund research and you learn the basic facts.
- Bill Gates

Market research studies are not cheap to conduct. Expecting too much from a low budget study is a sure shot way to fail most of the time. A lot of thought needs to be given while finalizing the budget for a market research study. Like, how much needs to be spent during exploratory phase and descriptive phase of the market research. You also need to have contingency fund in case you need to change something mid-course of the study (not advisable but sometime unavoidable) like, increasing number of interviews and focus groups to be conducted, regions or markets to be covered etc.

Lowering your budget might not attract good market research firms to respond to your RFP, resulting in sub-optimal outcome of the study. On the other hand, assigning large budget may result in poor returns from the research and may even limit number of future market research studies which can be conducted. Thus, you need to find a balance.

MISTAKE 4: RELYING TOO MUCH ON IN-HOUSE RESEARCH

Some people use research like a drunkard uses a lamp post, for support rather than for illumination.
−David Ogilvy

In-house research teams are situated too close to end-users, and thus are unlikely to produce fully transparent and objective market research studies. They are also affected by organization politics and most of the time end up supporting the point of view (POV) of their superiors and end users.

For example, sales department may request in-house research teams to conduct a market research to highlight issues related to common market conditions faced by their competitors as well just to convince the management that they are doing their best at sales and it's a market problem rather than their failure. Also, in-house teams tend to have myopic view of their industry as they are not always exposed to external variables.

An external market research agency has a far better chance to provide objective suggestions without any bias when it comes to; research design, data collection, analysis and other research suggestions. It doesn't mean in-house research teams are completely useless. They can be more effectively used during exploratory phase of research. Just don't rely on them too much for full-fledge research studies.

MISTAKE 5: CONSIDERING MARKET RESEARCH AS ONE-TIME ACTIVITY RATHER THAN A CONTINUOUS PROCESS

The more important reason is that the research itself provides an important long-run perspective on the issues that we face on a day-to-day basis.
-Ben Bernanke

Market research is an ongoing process, and usually one study leads to another study and new questions arise, where one is answered. Thinking that I have conducted one study and it's good enough for my organization is not the right way to approach market research.

The goal of market research is to reduce risk of decision making by providing actionable information in timely manner. Thus, committing to ongoing marketing research is a best strategy as this will keep providing answers, related to your product, services and markets as they evolve over time. Thus, helping you to maintain competitive edge in your industry.

MISTAKE 6: RELYING ON SINGLE DATA SOURCE

The goal is to transform data into information,
and information into insight.
- Carly Fiorina

Do not rely on single set of data no matter from where you have sourced it. This is especially true when you are collecting secondary research data. Let's consider a scenario where you are trying to assess market conditions, for your product and/or services in China, while doing desk research. You purchase a syndicated research report from one market research publisher on this topic and may think that I have got all the data I need. It is advisable that rather than relying too much on data provided by a single research report, you should procure multiple reports (ideally 4-5 reports) from different publishers. This will help you to compare the data offered by each publisher. You will also be able to verify this data by contacting those publishers or conducting dip-stick market research studies in-case of any variations in data.

Relying on a single set of data and/or source may lead you in wrong direction. Even during descriptive research phase, it is necessary to ensure multi-level (at the very least 3 levels) data checks during data collection phase of a study. This will reduce the risk of preparing research findings based on unreliable data.

MISTAKE 7: RELYING TOO MUCH ON FREE INTERNET INFORMATION

Doing research on the web is like using a library assembled piecemeal by pack rats and vandalized nightly.
- Roger Ebert

Whether to build questionnaires, define target audience or conducting desk research during exploratory research phase replying too much on information collected from search engines or online free website needs to be taken with a pinch of salt. The data needs to be cross checked with multiple authentic sources as mentioned in mistake # 6.

Sometimes you may be tempted to use free information given on the internet related to your proposed market research study. You may also assume that such information will answers all your questions. Unlike concrete suggestions made by a dedicated market research study, free information available on internet may not help you to take right decisions while solving your specific business problem. It's like taking medicines after doing Google search about symptoms of your illness. You may end up causing severe damage to your health, which can ultimately cost you much more than a professional doctor's fee.

MISTAKE 8: NOT INVOLVING YOUR MARKET RESEARCH AGENCY FROM THE BEGINNING

Our society needs more heroes who are scientists, researchers, and engineers. We need to celebrate and reward people who cure diseases, expand our understanding of humanity, and work to improve people's lives.
- Mark Zuckerberg

Quite often organizations try to force the research methodology to be used, survey questionnaires, data analysis tools while issuing their RFP for a market research study which may not be the ideal way to conduct that study. When asked about what made them decide about all this, most of the time their answer is on the lines, "Our CXO/VP/Managers want it done this way" or "We have decided this with our in-house research team" etc. This results in external agencies acting much more like in-house research teams and forced to take orders rather than helping you craft market research projects which meet your research objectives effectively.

To mitigate this, you need to select your market research agency based on their knowledge, experience and trust factor and then involve them in the research design process from the very beginning. This will result in streamlined, economical and effective market research study since the vendor will be able to make suggestions related to each aspect of market research, remove expensive design features and gear it to meet your research goals more effectively.

MISTAKE 9: FOCUSING ON POSITIVE DATA COLLECTION ONLY

Your most unhappy customers are your greatest source of learning.
- Bill Gates

Focusing on collecting positive data about your company, product or services often results in self-appeasement. Negative points are important as they tell you what you need to improve to become better than your competition. A well-designed research will help you gain insights about positives and negatives and quantify the impact they make on your customers.

MISTAKE 10: RELYING TOO MUCH ON ONLINE RESEARCH TOOLS

You can have data without information, but you cannot have information without data.
– Daniel Keys Moran

With the explosion of online surveys, panel discussion, focus groups etc. you may be tempted to use them thinking it can save you a lot of time and money (as they advertise). Most of the online survey tools are filled with professional respondents, who know how to get past survey screening questions. Also finding niche audience online to respond to your survey is near impossible.

For example, you can't expect to conduct a survey targeting high net worth individuals (HNIs) online related to a luxury brand. Lack of probing for open ended questions also is a major issue in online surveys, which can only be accomplished by a trained human interviewer. Online surveys can effectively be used while framing different hypothesis for research, or getting quick responses related to simple questions (like feedback surveys using 5, 7 or 10-point Likert scale).

MISTAKE 11: NOT LEARNING FROM PAST MARKET RESEARCH STUDIES

Predicting rain doesn't count; building arks does.
– Warren Buffet

It's not uncommon to see requests for market research studies made by organizations (often by newly joined employees) despite similar data collected previously. This happens either due to them not being aware of past study, or due to their excitement to spend their research budget to impress their superiors. It's important to note that conducting similar market research again is acceptable, only if all suggestions made in previous study were fully implemented and new study aims to build on those findings.

This situation can be avoided, if market research agencies are selected to build long-term partnerships. They will be able to get you more out of your research budget by avoiding redundant studies and suggesting improvements over previously conducted studies.

MISTAKE 12: OUTSOURCING MARKET RESEARCH STUDY TO A PROCUREMENT AGENCY

Money won't buy happiness, but it will pay the salaries of a large research staff to study the problem.
- Bill Vaughan

Outsourcing market research study to your procurement agency is the worst thing you can do to your research. Procurement agencies are inherently linear in their approach. Ultimately, they will end up asking multiple market research vendors to respond with set parameters defined by them.

This will result in no innovative suggestions being made by any market research agency. Also including them in the line of communication adds more challenges, for a market research agency to explain their research suggestions to you, and for you to convey your business problems and research objectives effectively. Procurement agency staff often have little knowledge about market research and thus they may take decisions solely based on most important factor for them i.e. cost of market research study. Eventually this will lead to your dissatisfaction with research outcome.

MISTAKE 13: TOO MUCH INSISTENCE ON TRACKING STUDIES

*There is a great difference between knowing and
understanding: you can know a lot about
something and not really understand it.*
- Charles F. Kettering

Tracking studies work successfully where market scenario changes very rapidly, for example in mobile manufacturing industry. In such a rapidly changing environment it's important to track consumer behavior, their satisfaction level, market share, competitors and new technology trends. It doesn't work when there are hardly any changes to the data, like in case of a pharma industry or traditional manufacturing industry.

Tracking studies by their very nature can become stale over time. This happens as the questions and objectives defined during commissioning of the tracking study remains almost same without any major changes. This is due to the need to provide consistent trend analysis by tracking study. Your product and/or services might change during tracking study along with business environment which may not get reflected in findings of a tracking study. This may wear you out, as you may feel that you are getting no benefit out of market research even after spending regularly.

Like all business processes, tracking studies needs to evolve to match your current research needs and this can only be possible through your constant supervision.

MISTAKE 14: HIRING TOO MANY MARKET RESEARCH AGENCIES TO CONDUCT SAME RESEARCH SIMULTANEOUSLY

Too many cooks spoil the broth.
- Proverb

Conducting same market research study using multiple market research agencies in same geography is not always advisable (except for some consumer studies e.g. new packaging study, pricing research, mystery shopping etc.).

You may think that this will help you avoid mistake mentioned in mistake # 6 but this may lead to wearing out respondent (if they are niche audiences like CXOs), producing confusing outcomes as each agency will have their own process to collect and analyze data and make your market research agencies feel less secure thus making them prone to avoid creative suggestions. This may also cause you to exhaust your research budget more quickly which may be needed for a follow up study.

MISTAKE 15: NOT BUILDING LONG TERM RELATIONSHIPS WITH YOUR MARKET RESEARCH VENDORS

The aim of marketing is to know and understand the customer so well, the product or service sells itself.
– Peter Drucker

Wherever possible it's always advisable to build long term relationships with your market research vendors. When hiring a lawyer or family doctor you expect them to know all the nuances about your legal/health issues, so that they can give best possible professional advice over a course of time. Similarly having long term relationships with your market research vendors can result in you getting best prices, accurate suggestions and even priority delivery schedules for your market research studies.

BONUS MISTAKE

Not involving your market research agency during implementation phase

You can tell whether a man is clever by his answers. You can tell whether a man is wise by his questions.
- Naguib Mahfouz

If you have read this far, you deserve to get a bonus suggestion. This may be the most important mistake you should avoid at all cost. Involving your market research vendors during implementation phase is advisable as they are the ones who have made these suggestions in the first place. They will be able to guide you about any obstacles, while trying to implement their suggestions. Implementing the findings of market research study is necessary for the success of your business. All the effort, time and money spent on a market research study will go to waste if you don't use it for solving your business problems.

I have highlighted these 15 market research mistakes to avoid from my experience, in hope that it will help you and your organization improve your returns on investment (ROI) from market research and keep you engaged with this awesome process.

- End -

ABOUT THE AUTHOR

Ambarish Verma is the founder of MarketResearchReports.com which is world's largest market research store offering quality market research, SWOT analysis, competitive intelligence and industry reports.

He has over a decade of experience in designing and implementing market research and have worked for a variety of industries. He is a serial entrepreneur with experience and exposure in market research, management consulting, digital marketing, ITeS and education fields. He likes sharing his experiences in the field of Market Research to those who are passionate and like exploring more about this field.

Entrepreneur, Explorer & Educator are the three words he uses to define himself.